My four Book

by Jane Belk Moncure

illustrated by Ellen Sasaki

SCHOLASTIC INC.

New York   Toronto   London   Auckland   Sydney
Mexico City   New Delhi   Hong Kong   Buenos Aires

This is Little four.

Little Four lives in the house of four.

The house of four . . .

has four rooms. Count them.

Every day Little  goes for a walk.

Sometimes he goes to the zoo.

At the zoo, Little  sees three monkeys in a tree . . .

and one monkey on the ground.

How many monkeys does he see?

He buys four bananas

for the monkeys.

How many bananas can he give each monkey?

Then Little  finds four balls on the path.

He sees four seals in the water.

He throws the first ball to the first seal.

Who catches the second ball?

The third seal catches the third ball.
Who catches the fourth ball?

Next Little  sees some baby lions.

How many does he see?

Happy, Little  claps his hands.

One baby lion runs and hides.
How many are left?

Little  hops to the kangaroo cage. "I see two kangaroos," he says.

Just then . . .

two baby kangaroos jump out
of their mamas' pockets.

Now how many kangaroos are there?

Suddenly Little  hears a loud growl.

It is coming from inside a cave.

Out come two big polar bears
and two baby bears.

How many bears does Little  see?

Excited, Little  four waves his hands.

How many baby bears run to hide?

Then he stands very, very still.

How many bears peek out?

Little  skips along. He finds . . .

four peanuts.

Guess who peeks out of a door?

Does each elephant get a peanut?

Just then Little  four sees his friend the zookeeper.

She has a picnic basket.

"Come and share my lunch," says his friend.
"I have . . .

two sandwiches . . .

and two apples."

How many things does she have to eat?

After lunch, the zookeeper says,
"Let's have a treat."

Guess what she buys for Little four?

How many scoops of ice cream does Little  get?

What does he say four times?

Little  found four of everything.

four monkeys

four bears

four baby lions

four elephants

four kangaroos

Now you find four things.

28

"See what I can do," says Little 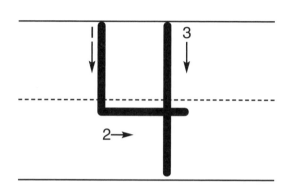.
He makes a 4 this way:

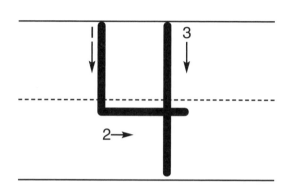

Then he makes the number word like this:

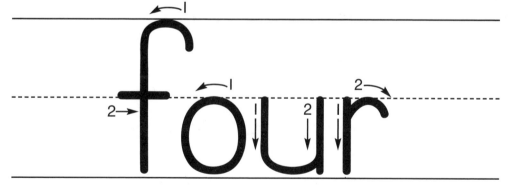

You can make them in the air with your finger.

1 2
5 6 7